WILD·WORLD·OF·ANIMALS

DESERTS

MICHAEL CHINERY
ILLUSTRATED BY DAVID WRIGHT

Kingfisher Books

Kingfisher Books, Grisewood & Dempsey Ltd,
Elsley House, 24-30 Great Titchfield Street,
London W1P 7AD

First published in 1991 by Kingfisher Books

BRITISH LIBRARY CATALOGUING IN PUBLICATION DATA
A catalogue record for this book is available from
the British Library

ISBN 0 86272 725 1

Series editor: Mike Halson
Series designer: Terry Woodley
Designer: Dave West Children's Books
Illustrators: David Wright (pp. 1, 4–37)
Eric Robson (pp. 2–3, 38)
Cover illustrations: John Butler

Phototypeset by Southern Positives and Negatives
(SPAN), Lingfield, Surrey.
Printed and bound by Cambus Litho Ltd, East Kilbride.

Contents

Life in the deserts

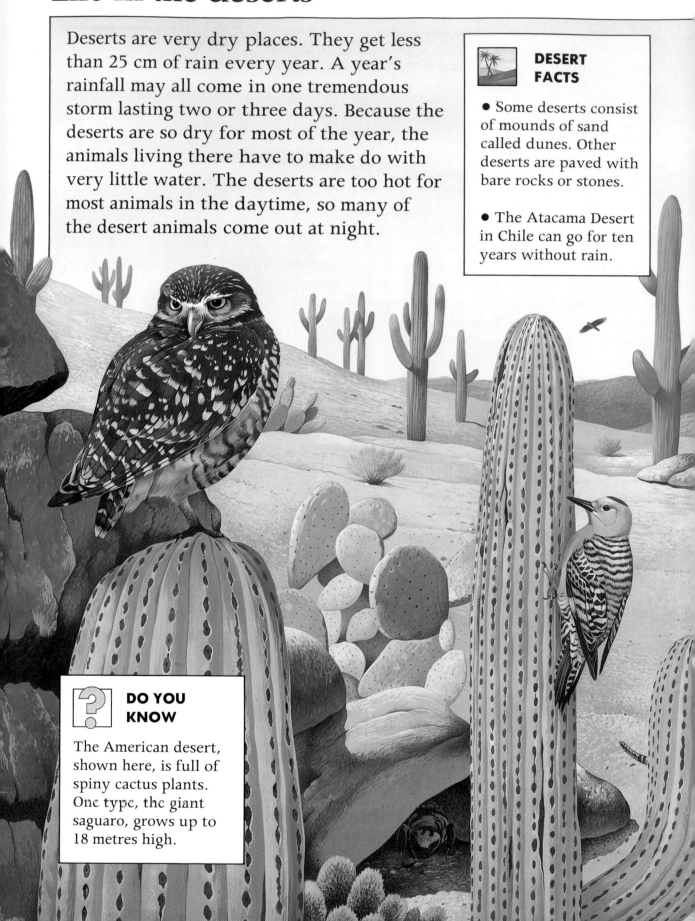

Deserts are very dry places. They get less than 25 cm of rain every year. A year's rainfall may all come in one tremendous storm lasting two or three days. Because the deserts are so dry for most of the year, the animals living there have to make do with very little water. The deserts are too hot for most animals in the daytime, so many of the desert animals come out at night.

DESERT FACTS

● Some deserts consist of mounds of sand called dunes. Other deserts are paved with bare rocks or stones.

● The Atacama Desert in Chile can go for ten years without rain.

? DO YOU KNOW

The American desert, shown here, is full of spiny cactus plants. One type, the giant saguaro, grows up to 18 metres high.

THE WORLD'S DESERTS

This map shows the world's deserts. Most of these are inland but some are to be found in coastal areas. Deserts form in places where the winds carry little moisture that can fall as rain. For example, the deserts of North America are dry because the winds have dropped their water over the Rockies, a chain of mountains running right down the west coast.

The Arabian camel

There are two kinds of camel – the Arabian with one hump and the Bactrian with two. (The Bactrian is shown on page 8.) Camels are perfectly designed for life in the dry, sandy deserts. An Arabian camel can last for several days without water, and can go for weeks without a drink if it has green plants to eat. It gets thin without water, but quickly returns to normal after drinking. It can drink over 100 litres in ten minutes!

Arabian camels roam the deserts of Arabia and North Africa in small groups. They eat the leaves of any trees and bushes they find.

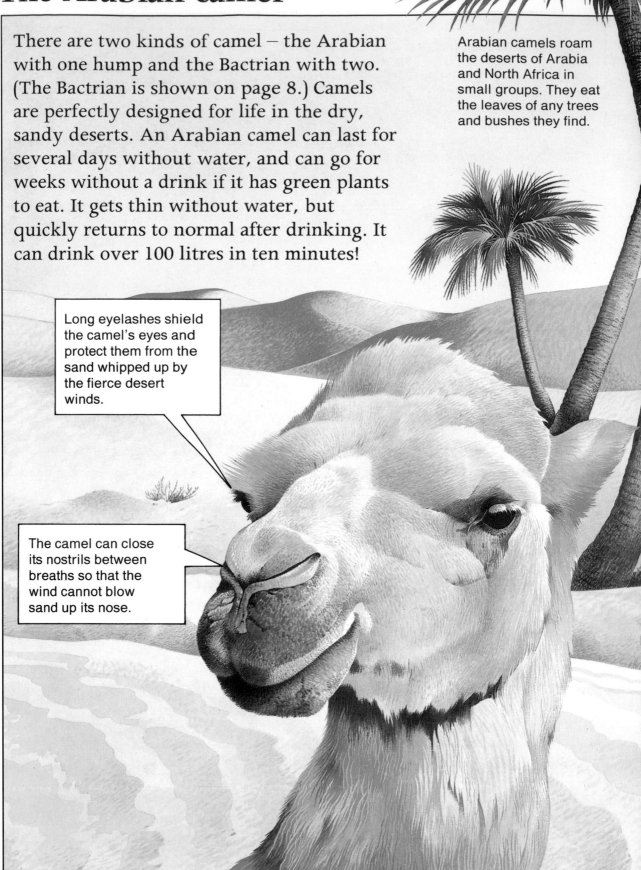

Long eyelashes shield the camel's eyes and protect them from the sand whipped up by the fierce desert winds.

The camel can close its nostrils between breaths so that the wind cannot blow sand up its nose.

The camel's hump is full of fat – a store of food in readiness for hard times. The hump shrinks as the food is gradually used up.

CAMEL FACTS

● The Arabian camel is about 3 metres long and is nearly 2 metres high at the shoulder.

● Camels used for riding are a breed of Arabian camels called dromedaries. A good riding camel can travel 150 km in a day.

Desert people have found all sorts of ways to use camels. They ride them, use them to carry goods, drink their milk and burn their dried dung as fuel! Arabian camels have been taken to deserts in several other parts of the world.

Broad feet help to spread the camel's weight and stop it from sinking into the loose sand.

The Bactrian – a camel with two humps

Camels with two humps are called Bactrian camels. They live in the cold deserts of Central Asia. Thick coats protect them from the cold. Like the one-humped camels of Arabia, they can go without food and water for long periods. Desert people domesticated, or tamed, the camels long ago so they could be used to carry goods and equipment.

BACTRIAN FACTS

● Bactrian camels are 2 metres high. They weigh about 500 kg when fully grown.

● Domesticated camels have more hair than wild ones and the hair is used to make warm blankets.

SURVIVAL WATCH

Truly wild Bactrian camels live only in the Gobi Desert. There are not many of them left now because people have killed lots of them for meat and leather. But there are still plenty of domesticated Bactrians.

People used to think that the two humps carried water, but they really contain stores of fat to keep the animals going when food is short.

Bactrians have thick winter coats. The fur falls out in big chunks in spring and the camels look very scruffy for a while.

The cunning ant-lion

Not many animals make traps to catch their food, but a creeping insect called an ant-lion does. It digs cone-shaped pits in the sand and hides at the bottom, waiting for other insects to fall in. It is called an ant-lion because most of the insects that fall into its trap are ants.

Ant-lion pits may be up to 5 cm deep and 8 cm wide at the top. Where there are large groups of these pits it can be difficult for insects to avoid them.

Not all ant-lions make pits. Some simply bury themselves in the sand. When they sense that an insect is near, they rush out from their hiding place and grab it

Ants lose their footing in the loose sand on the sides of the pit and start to slide down towards the waiting ant-lion,

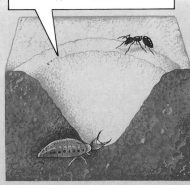

When the ant-lion senses that an ant has tumbled into its pit, it flicks up sand to knock the insect within reach of its spiky jaws.

? DO YOU KNOW

Ant-lions are actually young insects. When they grow up they turn into dainty winged insects like the one shown below. The adult ant-lions feed on insects plucked from plants.

The fennec – a little fox with big ears

The fennec is the world's smallest fox, but it is the one with the biggest ears. The fennec uses them to listen for the faint sounds made by the animals that it eats. It also uses them to listen for enemies, such as jackals and hyaenas. The large ears also act like radiators to keep the fennec cool. Blood flows through them, just as water flows through a radiator, and gives out heat so that the animal does not get too hot.

DO YOU KNOW

Fennecs do not need to drink, even in the driest desert. They get all the water they need from their food.

Fennecs have become very popular as pets.

FENNEC FACTS

● Fennecs live in the deserts of Africa and Arabia.

● The adult fennec's body is less than 40 cm long, but its ears are 15 cm long! Its bushy tail is about 25 cm long.

Fennecs avoid the hot sun by spending the daytime in burrows as much as 1 metre deep. The sand is much cooler there. The animals come out to hunt in the evening.

Insects and spiders make up much of the fennec's food, but they sometimes eat larger animals such as hares and gerbils.

The mother shows her cubs how to find food. The cubs' ears are short at first, but they grow quickly when the cubs start hunting.

The kit fox – a fennec look-alike

The kit fox lives in the American deserts, a long way from the fennec's African home. The two animals look alike because they live in exactly the same way. The kit fox spends the daytime in a deep burrow where the air is quite cool. It comes out at nightfall to hunt for small animals. Picking up their sounds with its huge ears, it dashes after them at high speed. It carries them back to the safety of its burrow to eat them.

SURVIVAL WATCH

Kit foxes are getting very rare. Many of them have been killed by poison put down to kill coyotes. Their homes are also being destroyed as towns spread into the desert.

Huge ears help the kit fox to stay cool. They also pick up every sound in the desert at night as the fox hunts for food.

The kit fox eats all sorts of small animals, including rabbits and lizards. This kangaroo rat is about to become its next meal.

KIT FOX FACTS

● Kit foxes live on the grassy plains as well as in the desert.

● The kit fox is up to about 90 cm long, including its bushy tail. It is also called the swift fox because it can run very fast.

The speedy oryx

Oryx are fast-running antelope found in the deserts of Africa and Arabia. The Arabian oryx pictured here is the smallest and rarest of the three different kinds. It lives in small herds in a few parts of the Arabian Desert. It feeds on scattered clumps of grass, usually early in the morning when there is some dew to provide extra moisture.

 SURVIVAL WATCH

The Arabian oryx almost died out in the 1960s. Fortunately, zoos have been able to breed them, but there may no longer be any oryx left in the wild.

Oryx herds gallop away when alarmed, but if the animals are cornered they put their heads down and attack with their long, sharp horns.

The horns of the Arabian oryx are about 75 cm long and almost straight. When seen from the side, the animal appears to have only one horn.

 ORYX FACTS

● Oryx herds consist mainly of females and their young. Most adult males live by themselves but they join their herds in the mating season.

The addax

The addax is a sturdy antelope that lives in some of the driest parts of the Sahara Desert. Small herds wander from place to place looking for fresh grass. Fresh leaves grow quickly after brief showers and the addax has a wonderful ability to smell the new leaves from a distance. Addaxes can go without water for long periods, and some of them probably never drink at all. They get all the water they need from the grass.

SURVIVAL WATCH

The addax used to be common in the deserts of North Africa and Arabia, but it has now become a very rare animal because people hunt it for its skin and its long spiral horns. Another problem is caused by the herds of goats which also graze in the desert and eat the grass that the addax needs.

The addax is 1 metre high at the shoulder. Its coat is greyish in winter and white or sandy in the summer.

The hooves are very broad and allow the addax to walk or run easily over loose sand without sinking too far down into it.

The jumping jerboa

Jerboas are built for jumping. They bound along on their long back legs just like miniature kangaroos. Several kinds of jerboas live in the deserts of Africa and Asia. Like most small desert animals, they hide in underground burrows during the day and come out to feed at night. Jerboas feed mainly on seeds and leaves, but they also eat beetles and other insects. They use their short front legs for picking up food.

JERBOA FACTS

● Jerboas have excellent hearing and eyesight and a superb sense of smell.

● Jerboas are able to leap 1 metre or more up into bushes to grab juicy leaves.

Even in its burrow the jerboa is not always safe from its enemies. Sometimes a snake will slither inside in search of a meal.

The jerboa's hind legs are four times as long as its front legs and they enable it to travel in huge leaps of up to 3 metres at a time.

As soon as the jerboa realizes that it is in danger, it explodes out of the other end of the tunnel in a spray of sand.

The kangaroo rat

The kangaroo rat is the American equivalent of the jerboa. It looks just like a tiny kangaroo as it leaps over the desert floor at night. Its main enemies are owls and snakes. The kangaroo rat feeds mainly on grass and seeds.

? DO YOU KNOW

Kangaroo rats often spread from the deserts to farmland. There they do a lot of damage by digging up newly planted crops.

The Mongolian gerbil

Also known as a jird, the Mongolian gerbil comes from the deserts of Central Asia. It lives in huge colonies, and is active by day and night. If alarmed, the gerbil warns its neighbours by thumping the ground with its big hind feet.

? DO YOU KNOW

Gerbils make fine pets. They love to sit up and look around them – just as they do when looking out for danger in the wild. Pet gerbils live for up to five years.

Gerbils hold their food in their dainty front paws. They have long back legs, but Mongolian gerbils are not good jumpers.

15

The dainty dorcas gazelle

This little antelope is only 60 cm high at the shoulder, but it can run at 80 km/h. It lives in the dry grasslands and deserts that stretch from West Africa to India. It feeds on roots and leaves and often gets all the water it needs from this food.

The dorcas gazelle is also called the jebeer. It is a rare animal and is in great danger of extinction in all of the areas where it lives.

 DO YOU KNOW

In North Africa the dorcas gazelle is very pale brown with straight horns, but in India it has a rich brown coat and its horns are more curved.

The wild ass – a desert donkey

Wild asses live in Africa and Asia. They can survive for many days without drinking, but when they do find water they can drink over 50 litres in just a few minutes. These animals were the ancestors of our domestic donkeys.

SURVIVAL WATCH

Only a few wild asses survive in Asia. In Africa there are probably no really wild asses left at all. The asses that do live there are almost certainly donkeys that have gone wild.

Piles of rocks can offer welcome shade from the scorching heat of the Sun.

Squabbling ground squirrels

Squirrels do not all live in trees. Many live in burrows in the ground. They are called ground squirrels. Several kinds live in the hot deserts of California and South Africa. They can stand higher temperatures than most other small mammals and are active during the daytime, but they still need to shelter from the midday Sun. Ground squirrels live in colonies, and hundreds of animals may share a network of tunnels.

? DO YOU KNOW

Squirrel tails have many uses. Tree squirrels use them to help change direction, while many ground squirrels use them for signalling. Squirrels in cold areas wrap their tails around them to keep warm, and desert squirrels use them as sunshades.

During the daytime the ground squirrels sit with their backs to the Sun and use their bushy tails as sun-shades to keep their bodies cool.

? DO YOU KNOW

Desert-living ground squirrels feed mainly on seeds and insects.

Ground squirrels often squabble during the morning and evening. It is too hot to fight in the middle of the day.

When the desert gets too hot, the squirrels look for shade. They go into their burrows or hide among rocks, where they cool down quite quickly.

The sandgrouse – a flying water carrier

The sandgrouse is a real expert in desert survival. It nests in the stony deserts of Africa and Asia and can raise a family in much drier places than other birds. Its secret is that the male birds use their fluffy breast feathers like sponges to soak up water and carry it back to their chicks. Some birds fly over 100 kilometres every day just to find water and take it back to their nests.

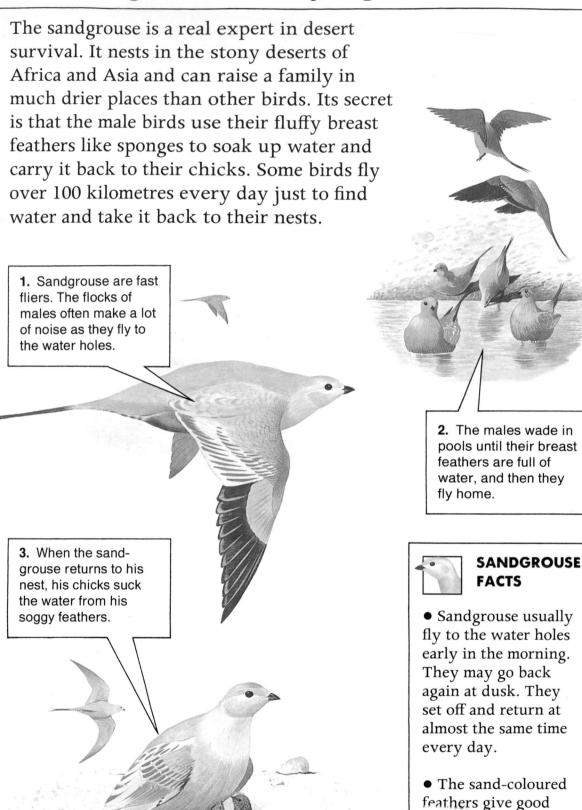

1. Sandgrouse are fast fliers. The flocks of males often make a lot of noise as they fly to the water holes.

2. The males wade in pools until their breast feathers are full of water, and then they fly home.

3. When the sand-grouse returns to his nest, his chicks suck the water from his soggy feathers.

SANDGROUSE FACTS

● Sandgrouse usually fly to the water holes early in the morning. They may go back again at dusk. They set off and return at almost the same time every day.

● The sand-coloured feathers give good desert camouflage.

The ferocious camel spider

For their size, the camel spiders have some of the most powerful jaws in the whole animal world. And they have appetites to match. They will go on eating until they are so full that they can hardly move. A single camel spider can eat over 100 small flies in 24 hours. Camel spiders feed mainly on insects, including tough-skinned beetles, but they will also eat scorpions, lizards and even small birds.

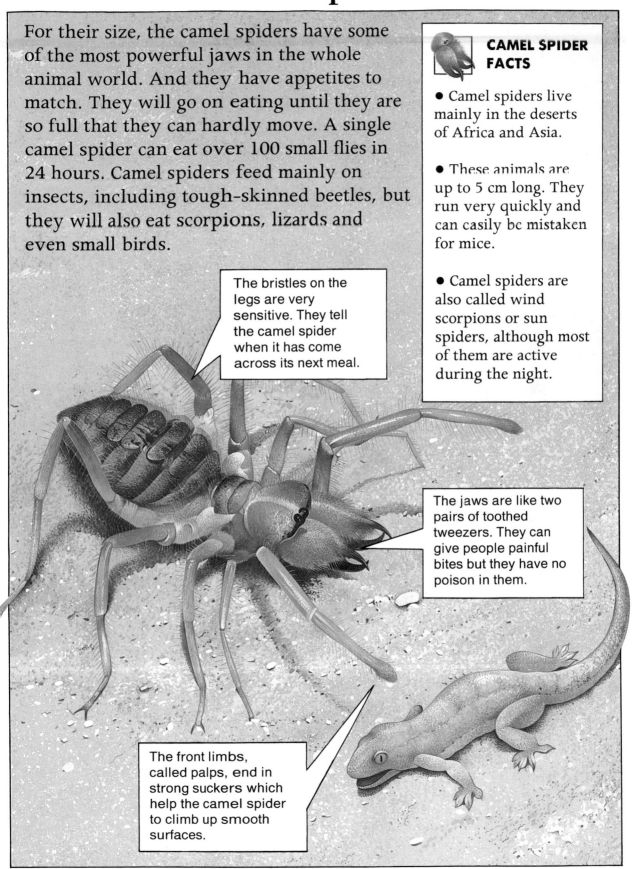

CAMEL SPIDER FACTS

● Camel spiders live mainly in the deserts of Africa and Asia.

● These animals are up to 5 cm long. They run very quickly and can easily be mistaken for mice.

● Camel spiders are also called wind scorpions or sun spiders, although most of them are active during the night.

The bristles on the legs are very sensitive. They tell the camel spider when it has come across its next meal.

The jaws are like two pairs of toothed tweezers. They can give people painful bites but they have no poison in them.

The front limbs, called palps, end in strong suckers which help the camel spider to climb up smooth surfaces.

The dancing scorpion

You can recognize a scorpion by its big claws and its slender tail. The tail is usually curled forward and it has a sting at the end. Some scorpions can kill people with their stings, but they do not usually sting unless they are annoyed. Most scorpions live in hot areas and many kinds live in the deserts. They walk slowly in search of food at night. Insects and spiders are their main foods, but large scorpions also eat lizards and mice. The food is crushed to pulp, and then sucked into the scorpion's tiny mouth.

SCORPION FACTS

● There are about 650 different kinds of scorpions. The biggest ones are about 20 cm long. Only a few are really dangerous.

● Some scorpions can survive without food for over a year.

● Scorpions have been known to survive being frozen in ice for several weeks on end.

Courting scorpions go dancing. The male holds his partner with his claws and the two animals move jerkily around until they are ready to mate. Males who do not dance properly may well get stung.

The scorpion's small eyes cannot see very well. The animal relies mainly on touch and smell to find out what is going on in the area around it.

The sting is a hard spine. Its poison is made in the swelling at its base. The sting is used mainly in self-defence.

Baby scorpions ride on their mother's back for two or three weeks and then gradually drop off. They have to look after themselves after that.

DO YOU KNOW

The desert scorpion has sensitive bristles all over its legs. These point in all directions and pick up vibrations from the movement of other creatures. The vibrations tell the scorpion where it might find something to eat.

Vibrations

Scorpions eat insects and other animals, which they catch with their claws. They use their stings only if the prey struggles a lot.

The sand cat

Sand cats live in the deserts of North Africa and Arabia. Their yellowish or greyish brown fur helps to camouflage them against the sand as they stalk their prey.

Hairy soles give the sand cat's feet a good grip on the loose desert sand.

The head is broad and flat, allowing the cat to hide behind quite small rocks.

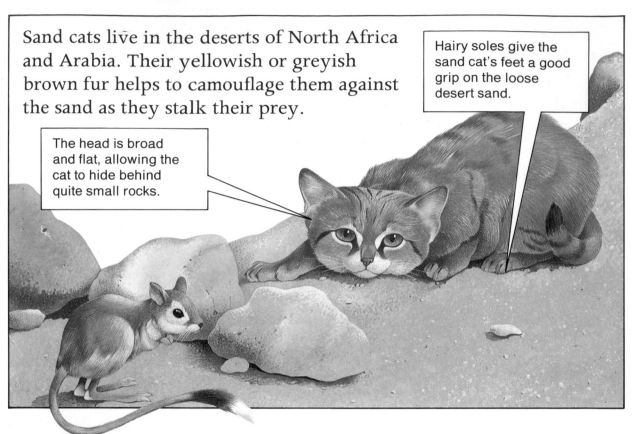

The golden mole

Golden moles look like balls of silky fur. They spend most of their time 'swimming' through the sand, pushing up ridges wherever they go. They are found only in southern Africa, and they feed mainly on insects and lizards.

A tough pad of skin protects the mole's nostrils while it is burrowing. Its legs are so short that you can hardly see them.

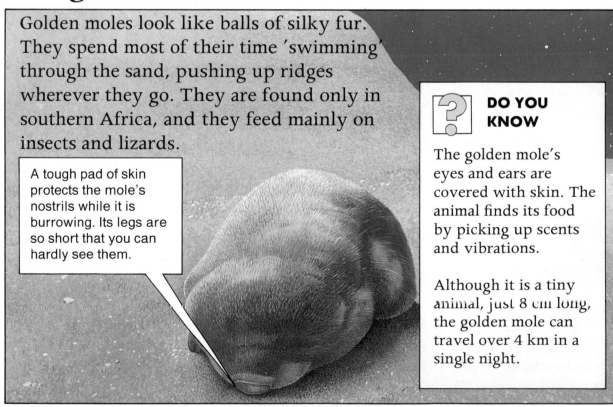

? DO YOU KNOW

The golden mole's eyes and ears are covered with skin. The animal finds its food by picking up scents and vibrations.

Although it is a tiny animal, just 8 cm long, the golden mole can travel over 4 km in a single night.

The caracal – a high-flying cat

The caracal is one of the world's fastest cats. It catches hares and small antelope. It can also charge at a flock of birds and catch several of them before they can take off. And the birds are not safe even if they do manage to take off, because the caracal can leap into the air and catch them. Even eagles can be caught by this amazing cat. Caracals live around the edges of the deserts of Africa, Arabia, and India.

? DO YOU KNOW

The caracal's black ear-tufts are used as signals. The animals have to be quiet when hunting and the young caracals watch their mother's ears to know what to do.

The caracal has long legs and is a superb high-jumper. It can leap 2 metres into the air to take birds by surprise.

Powerful paws can kill a bird with one blow, knocking it to the ground or sweeping it straight into the caracal's mouth.

CARACAL FACTS

• The caracal is about 60 cm long and up to 45 cm high at the shoulder. It weighs up to 15 kg.

• Caracals can run at more than 50 km/h over short distances.

The bearded lizard

The bearded lizard, also called the bearded dragon, is named for the bristly shield on its throat. It is about 60 cm long and lives in the Australian deserts. It spends a lot of time sitting in the sun and likes to bask in the late afternoon sunshine. By doing this its body stays warm through the evening, so it can go on looking for food long after other lizards have cooled down and gone to sleep. It feeds mainly on insects.

? DO YOU KNOW

The bearded lizard can run on its hind legs. This helps to cool its body by lifting it clear of the hot ground.

On hot ground, the lizard often cools its feet by lifting each foot in turn.

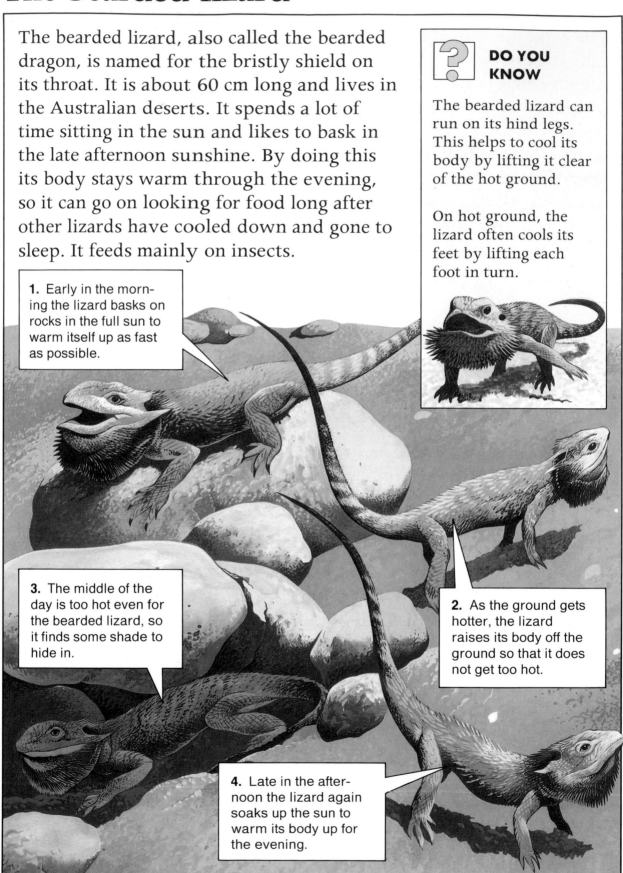

1. Early in the morning the lizard basks on rocks in the full sun to warm itself up as fast as possible.

3. The middle of the day is too hot even for the bearded lizard, so it finds some shade to hide in.

2. As the ground gets hotter, the lizard raises its body off the ground so that it does not get too hot.

4. Late in the afternoon the lizard again soaks up the sun to warm its body up for the evening.

The spadefoot toad

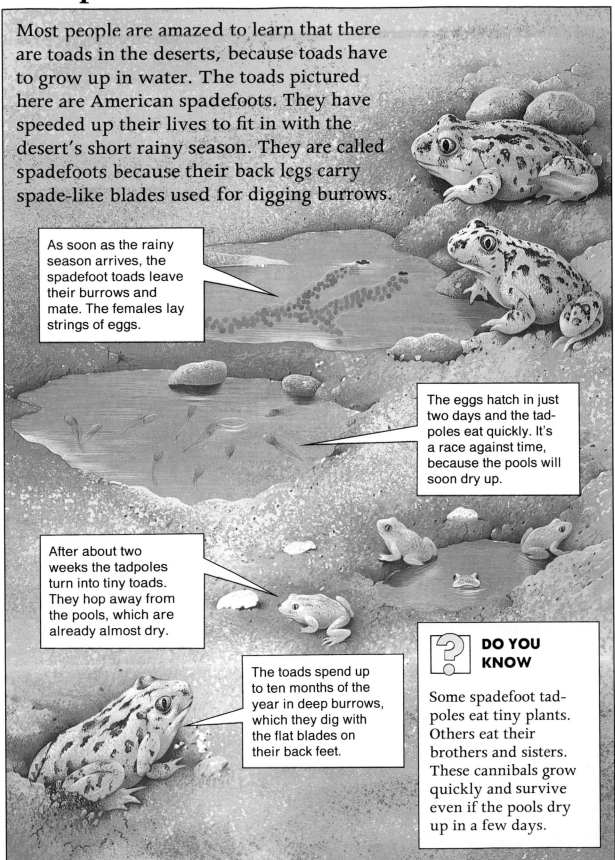

Most people are amazed to learn that there are toads in the deserts, because toads have to grow up in water. The toads pictured here are American spadefoots. They have speeded up their lives to fit in with the desert's short rainy season. They are called spadefoots because their back legs carry spade-like blades used for digging burrows.

As soon as the rainy season arrives, the spadefoot toads leave their burrows and mate. The females lay strings of eggs.

The eggs hatch in just two days and the tadpoles eat quickly. It's a race against time, because the pools will soon dry up.

After about two weeks the tadpoles turn into tiny toads. They hop away from the pools, which are already almost dry.

The toads spend up to ten months of the year in deep burrows, which they dig with the flat blades on their back feet.

DO YOU KNOW

Some spadefoot tadpoles eat tiny plants. Others eat their brothers and sisters. These cannibals grow quickly and survive even if the pools dry up in a few days.

The thorny devil

The thorny devil is a slow-moving lizard from the sandy deserts of Australia. It need not move quickly because it is protected from attack by its prickles. Dew forming on the lizard's spines at night provides it with drinking water.

THORNY DEVIL FACTS

- The thorny devil is only about 15 cm long.

- The devil can pick up 40 ants in a minute and can eat 1000 of them in a single meal.

The frilled lizard

The frilled lizard is a fraud. When it is frightened it spreads its broad collar and pretends to be much bigger and fiercer than it really is. This display scares its enemies away. Frilled lizards live in the deserts and dry grasslands of Australia.

The frill contains stiff rods, rather like an umbrella. The lizard makes a loud hissing noise, and this makes it seem even fiercer.

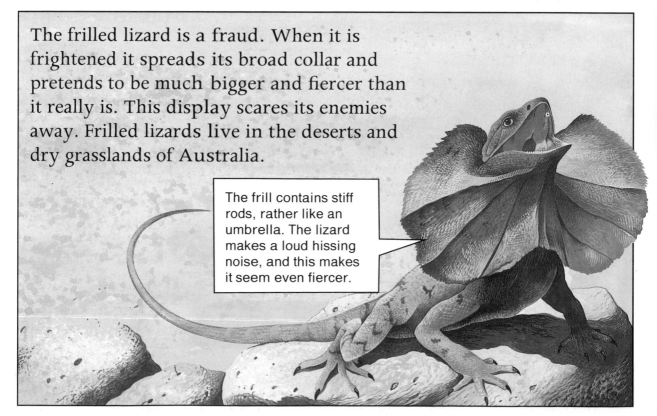

The poisonous gila monster

This plump, slow-moving lizard lives in the deserts of North America. It has a poisonous bite and its bright colours warn other animals to leave it alone. It feeds mainly on birds' eggs and other small animals.

The lizard stores food in its fat tail. The food keeps the lizard going through the dry season.

GILA MONSTER FACTS

● The gila monster is up to about 60 cm long and is active mainly in the wet season.

● This rare animal is now protected by law.

Like most lizards, the monster tracks down its food by flicking its tongue out to pick up the scent of its prey.

The chuckwalla

Chuckwalla lizards live in North America's rocky deserts. They eat the desert flowers in spring and early summer and sleep for the rest of the year. If alarmed, the lizard dives into a rock crevice and pumps its body up with air so that it cannot be pulled out.

CHUCKWALLA FACTS

● The chuckwalla is up to 45 cm long and weighs about 1.5 kg.

● It sleeps for seven months of the year.

Deadly desert rattlesnakes

Several kinds of rattlesnakes, or rattlers, live in the deserts of North America. They get their name for the rattling or hissing noise they make with their tails when they are disturbed. The rattle warns larger animals to keep away, for the rattler does not want to waste its poison on animals that are too large for it to eat. It feeds on kangaroo rats and other small mammals at night. Although they have poisonous bites, rattlesnakes are eaten by other snakes, by the roadrunner bird, and even by people.

DO YOU KNOW

A rattlesnake can track down its prey in total darkness with the aid of a heat-sensitive pit on each side of its head. Nerves in these pits pick up the warmth of the prey and tell the snake exactly where the prey is to be found.

RATTLESNAKE FACTS

● There are about 30 different kinds of rattlesnakes, but they do not all live in the deserts. The biggest rattlesnakes are over 2 metres long.

Heat-sensitive pits on its head tell the rattlesnake when it is getting close to its warm-blooded prey.

SIDEWINDER TRACKS

The small sidewinder rattlesnake has a clever way of moving over loose sand. It throws its body into loops and almost rolls along. Only two points of its body touch the sand at any one time, leaving parallel tracks in the sand.

The fangs swing forward when the snake opens its mouth ready to strike, and they inject deadly poison into the prey.

Each time a rattler changes its skin it adds a new ring to its rattle. This means that the rattle gets bigger and louder as the snake gets older.

The pack rat

The pack rat of the American desert spends much of its life scampering over prickly cacti, so it has to mind where it puts its feet. It nests in cactus clumps and makes its nest even safer by piling other bits of cactus all round it. There are several grass-lined rooms in the nest and the pack rat sleeps here during the day.

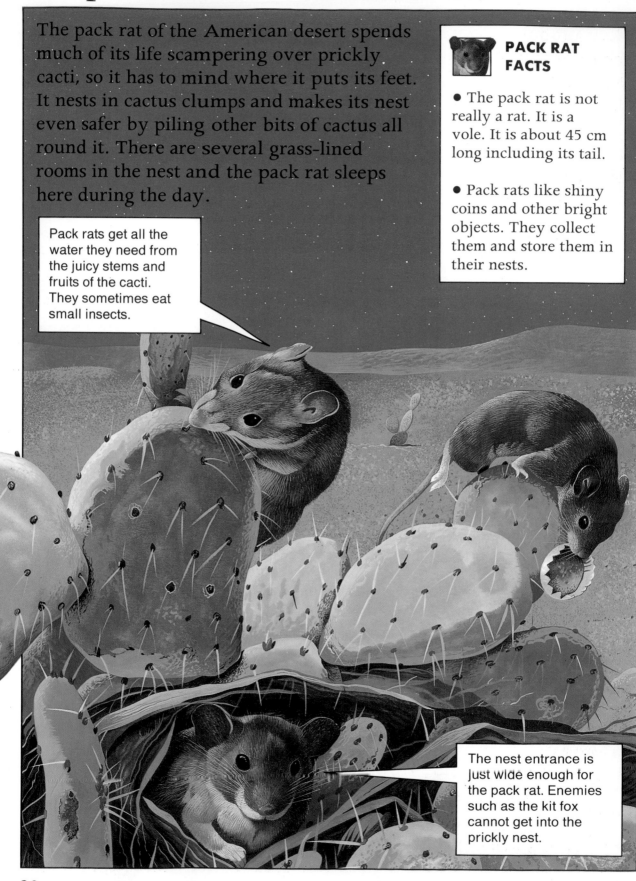

PACK RAT FACTS

● The pack rat is not really a rat. It is a vole. It is about 45 cm long including its tail.

● Pack rats like shiny coins and other bright objects. They collect them and store them in their nests.

Pack rats get all the water they need from the juicy stems and fruits of the cacti. They sometimes eat small insects.

The nest entrance is just wide enough for the pack rat. Enemies such as the kit fox cannot get into the prickly nest.

The long-eared jack rabbit

Jack rabbits are actually hares. They have much longer legs and ears than true rabbits. Several kinds live in North America. The black-tailed jack rabbit pictured here lives in the deserts. It does not burrow and avoids the daytime heat by sitting in the shade of a cactus or a rock. Its huge ears help it to keep cool.

Desert jack rabbits have extra-large ears. Blood flowing through the ears gives off heat to the air and this helps to cool the jack rabbit down.

The jack rabbit eats desert plants at night. Its large ears are then used to pick up the sounds made by any approaching enemies.

JACK RABBIT FACTS

● The jack rabbit is about 60 cm long. Its ears are 20 cm long.

● The animal can run at 70 km/h and can leap up to 6 metres.

● Jack rabbit babies can walk as soon as they are born.

The gila woodpecker

There are not many trees in the desert, so the gila woodpecker has to make do with the tree-shaped giant saguaro cacti. These cacti grow to about 18 metres high in the American deserts and provide food and shelter for many animals. The gila woodpecker feeds mainly on beetles and other insects. It nests in neat holes which it digs in the stems with its sturdy beak.

SURVIVAL WATCH

The gila woodpecker has few enemies and is not in any direct danger, but its home is under threat. The saguaro cactus, which takes about 200 years to reach its full size, is dying out in some of the desert areas.

DO YOU KNOW

You can tell a male gila woodpecker from a female because only the male has a red cap.

The wounded flesh of the nest hole forms a sort of scab and becomes quite dry, so the hole makes a comfortable nest for the woodpecker and its chicks. Few enemies can reach the nest.

The gila woodpecker supports itself with its stiff tail feathers while clinging to the stem of the cactus.

Backward and forward facing toes give the woodpecker's clawed feet a really secure grip on the side of the saguaro.

The elf owl

Elf owls live in the American deserts, especially in parts where the saguaro cacti grow. The birds fly at night and spend the daytime resting in holes in the cacti. They usually use old woodpecker nests.

The large eyes of the elf owl help the bird to see its insect prey in the dark.

ELF OWL FACTS

- The elf owl is only about 13 cm long and is one of the world's smallest owls. It feeds on insects, spiders and scorpions.

The burrowing owl

Burrowing owls live on the plains and in the deserts of North America. They fly by day and spend the night in underground burrows. They can dig their own holes, but prefer burrows dug by other animals.

Burrowing owls are about 20 cm long and have longer legs than most other owls. They eat insects and other small animals.

SURVIVAL WATCH

Burrowing owls are now rare on the plains because farming destroys their nests. And in the deserts they are at risk from the spread of towns.

The remarkable roadrunner

The roadrunner lives in some of the hottest parts of the American deserts. It has short wings and does not fly very much. The bird is 50–60 cm long and feeds mainly on insects and scorpions. It also catches lizards and snakes and crushes them with its strong feet before eating them. The roadrunner hunts early in the morning and in the evening. It keeps cool in the middle of the day by sitting in the shade of rocks or cacti.

DO YOU KNOW

The roadrunner is a member of the cuckoo family, although it builds its own nest. It got its name from its habit of running next to horse-drawn wagons and eating the insects disturbed by the horses' hooves.

The roadrunner normally runs at about 25 km/h, but has a top speed of 40 km/h. It uses its wings to keep its balance.

The roadrunner often builds its nest in cactus bushes, where it is safe from most of its enemies. It lays up to six eggs.

The mourning dove

Mourning doves can live in very hot and dry conditions and they sometimes nest in the hottest parts of the American deserts. But they still need water and may fly 100 km or more every day to drink. These birds also live in towns and on farmland.

Mourning doves often nest on prickly cacti. They do not mind the Sun's heat beating down on them.

 MOURNING DOVE FACTS

- The mourning dove is about 25 cm long and is a very fast flier.

- The dove is named for its sad, cooing call. Its wings make a whistling sound in flight.

The desert tortoise

Desert tortoises are up to 35 cm long and live in the American deserts. They feed mainly on cacti. As long as they have juicy cacti to eat they do not need to drink, even in the dry season. They store water from the cacti in their bodies.

SURVIVAL WATCH

Desert tortoises are now rare because thousands have been collected and sold as pets. Laws now protect these animals so they may increase again in the wild.

Tortoises have sharp-edged horny jaws instead of teeth. These tough jaws can munch through prickly cacti without harm.

Harvester ants

Harvester ants live in many of the drier parts of the world and they feed mainly on seeds. Worker ants stream out from their nests every day and bring back seeds from as far as 100 metres away. Large-headed workers, often called soldiers, crack the seeds open with their large jaws. The soft kernels are stored in special chambers in the nest. The husks are thrown out and often form a large mound around the nest entrance.

DO YOU KNOW

The ants in each nest collect millions of seeds in a year, mostly at the end of the wet season. The stored seeds keep the ants going through the dry season, when food is scarce. The seeds do not sprout in the nest because it is too dry.

Workers looking for seeds take the same routes from their nest every day. Their tiny feet gradually make clear paths.

Ants can carry seeds larger than their own bodies, and they can hurry along with them at speeds of over 2 metres per minute.

Large-headed workers open seeds all day long, usually just inside the nest. Other ants take the kernels to the storerooms.

Honey pot ants

Honey pot ants live in the American and Australian deserts and feed mainly on nectar from flowers. As the flowers bloom only for a short time after rain, the ants have developed a way of storing the nectar for use in the dry season. Some of the ants in the colony turn themselves into living 'honey pots'. Workers pass nectar to the honey pots, whose bodies gradually swell up. When the other ants are hungry in the dry season the honey pots feed them with the nectar.

The honey pots start to fill up with nectar as soon as they have grown up, while their skins are still soft and stretchy. Some kinds of honey pot ants store fruit juices instead of nectar.

A worker returning to the nest passes its load of nectar through its mouth into the mouth of a honey pot for safe keeping.

Honey pot ants make their nests deep in the ground. They sometimes go down as much as 5 metres below the surface.

The honey pot cannot move and spends all its life hanging from the roof of the nest. It is about as big as a pea when full.

DO YOU KNOW

Honey pot ant nests may contain up to 1500 living honey pots, all of them bulging with sweet nectar.

Australian aborigines – the native people of Australia – dig up the honey pots and eat them like sweets.

Deserts in danger

Deserts are harsh places and not many people live there. Even so, we are still damaging many deserts. Farms and even towns are spreading into the American deserts, thanks to huge irrigation schemes bringing water to the dry areas. Mining is taking place in many areas to extract valuable minerals. Much of the world's oil lies under the deserts, especially in the Middle East, and oil wells cover thousands of hectares of desert.

Tourists often enjoy the strange desert landscape, but too many tourists will destroy the desert's delicate plant and animal life.

BRAND NEW DESERTS

Some deserts are actually growing, especially in parts of Africa. A decrease in rainfall in these areas is one reason for this. People are also to blame. They let too many sheep and goats graze on the thin grass. The plants are killed and the wind blows the topsoil away. All that is left is a dry, dusty landscape – a desert. It does not take long to turn grassland or even woodland into desert in a dry climate.

Useful words

Bask   To warm up the body by sitting in the heat of the Sun.

Cactus   Any of the many spiny plants of the American deserts. Their leafless stems are like barrels or pipes and they are used to store water. As the water is used up during the dry season the stems shrink and become deeply grooved. The plural of cactus is cacti.

Camouflage   To camouflage something is to colour it so that it is not easily seen, especially by an enemy. Animals use many forms of camouflage to trick their enemies. Some use camouflage to avoid being caught, while others use it to take their victims by surprise.

Colony   A group of animals that live closely together and help each other. Each member of the colony usually has a particular job.

Desert   A region that receives less than 25 cm of rain in a year. The deserts cover about one seventh of the Earth's land area. The biggest desert is the Sahara, in North Africa. It covers about 9 million square kilometres – nearly as much as the entire United States of America.

Dew   Water produced from moisture in the air when the air cools down at night. The cold air cannot hold as much moisture as warm air, so it drops it as dew on the ground and on low-growing plants.

Domestic   Not wild. Domesticated animals have been tamed by people for various purposes.

Extinction   The dying out of any kind of plant or animal. An extinct creature is one that no longer lives anywhere on Earth.

Fangs   The large teeth of a snake that inject poison into its prey.

Herd   The name given to any large group of hoofed animals, such as antelope, that live and feed together.

Husk   The tough, outer coat of a seed.

Insect   A small animal with six legs and a body that has three sections. Ant-lions and ants are insects but spiders and scorpions, which both have eight legs, are not.

Kernel   The soft, inner part of a seed, which normally grows into a new plant.

Mammal   Any animal that feeds its babies with milk from the mother's body. Several types of mammals live in the deserts, from the tiny kangaroo rat to the much larger camel.

Nature reserve   An area set aside to protect wild plants and animals – often rare ones that are in danger of dying out.

Prey   Any animal that is caught and eaten by another animal. Animals that hunt for prey are called predators.

Stalk   To stalk something – usually prey – is to creep up on it slowly and silently.

Tadpole   The young stage in the life of a frog or toad. Tadpoles live in water, but they grow up to become air-breathing animals living out of the water.

Vibration   A slight movement of the air or ground, often caused by something moving nearby.

Water hole   A pond where animals regularly gather to drink.

Index